Swords and Shadows

Navigating Youth Amidst the Wiles of Satan

Written by
Charles D. Fraune

Swords and Shadows:
Navigating Youth Amidst the Wiles of Satan

Charles D. Fraune, M.A.

Charles D. Fraune
2019

An original work by Charles D. Fraune, published in 2019.

Unless otherwise noted, all other quotes of Sacred Scripture are from the RSVCE.

Cover art: James Tissot, *Jesus Carried up to a Pinnacle of the Temple*, Brooklyn Museum.

Retreat Box Press. www.TheRetreatBox.com

Second printing 2019

Dedication

To Our Lady of Sorrows,
and to the glorious and triumphant Archangel,
Saint Michael.

Table of Contents

Introduction

"This is your hour, and the power of darkness."[1]

These are the words of Our Lord to those who came against Him to arrest Him in the Garden of Gethsemane. There is a real darkness in this world. It is not simply the darkness of doubt and despair in our minds, though this is one dimension. This real darkness is an army of spiritual beings, led by the one with whom Our Lord engaged in battle and conquered: Satan.

When you read the Gospel, you see it is filled with Our Lord's battle against Satan and these demons. The life of the Church, as clearly seen in the lives of the greatest Saints, is also filled with this battle. Today, exorcists, and all priests, see this activity of the evil one. Satan is real, but he has been conquered. Until the end, though, he is permitted to continue his activity.

Satan's activity today is, in a particular way, aimed at the youth. Young Catholics often feel oppressed by a culture of busyness, distractions, entertainments, bankrupt philosophies, and moral depravity unlike prior generations. It is not fair, and it is not the fault of the youth that they are in this situation. However, immersed in a culture without God, young Catholics can become weak and wounded and confused.

I was no different. The experiences of my childhood led me into a major depression and anxiety disorder that, among other things, caused me to leave the Faith and drop out of college. I had no weapons, no "sword of the Spirit,"[2] with which to fight and scatter the darkness and the shadows. But then Our Lord broke into my life and, through His Church, provided me with this sword and a map to navigate the way out.

The plight of the youth is why I wrote this book: to share what I have seen, experienced, and learned about this war.

The Church which Jesus Christ has instituted has perfected the art of spiritual warfare and is constantly training new soldiers. Learn to see how Satan acts and attacks and resist him. Take up the weapons of Holy Mother Church. Wait no longer. **Fight, and be free.**

---

[1] Luke 22:53
[2] Ephesians 6:17

Chapter One

Encroaching Shadows

Submit yourselves therefore to God.
Resist the devil and he will flee from you.
Draw near to God and he will draw near to you.
James 4:7

I renounce Satan…and all his works…and all his empty show.
I renounce Satan, the author and prince of sin.
I renounce sin, so as to live in the freedom of the children of God.
I renounce the lure of evil, so that sin may have no mastery over me.

I believe in God, the Father almighty, Creator of heaven and earth.
I believe in Jesus Christ, His only Son, Our Lord, who was born of the
Virgin Mary, suffered death and was buried, rose again from the dead
and is seated at the right hand of the Father.
I believe in the Holy Spirit, the holy Catholic Church, the communion
of Saints, the forgiveness of sins, the resurrection of the body, and life
everlasting. Amen.

Though I proclaim this now, this was not always the case for me.

The devil is real, as are the countless demons that work with him in the effort to seduce us away from love and obedience toward God. He tempts us through lies from others, which we believe, friendships where evil is celebrated, drugs, music where evil is celebrated and, most powerfully, through the desire to guide ourselves through life without God in it.

This book on spiritual warfare will pivot from the true story of my conversion, which can only be described as an act of God, rescuing a captive from the snares of the devil, and raising him up to be a spiritual warrior in the service of Christ the King. So, let's begin there.

It goes back to when I was five years old, when I was told, by other kids, that I was weird. What made me weird was the idea that I had big ears. I can recall, still to this day, the moment when I was five years old in the preschool library standing next to my mom, as two boys, about ten feet from me, were looking at me, pointing and laughing…at my ears. What made this particularly problematic is the way I reacted to it, which is relevant all throughout my life: I believed them. I not only believed that my ears were big, but that this little imperfection was what defined me. As a result, I expected others to tease me about it, and I began to loathe and hate my appearance. My dad tried to comfort me by reminding me that Dumbo also had big ears. That didn't quite work. Dumbo could also fly, but I could not!

Despite the efforts of my parents, I internalized this and entered on a path of self-loathing and self-pity. I began having nightmares that involved people cutting off my ears. I remember conversations, not in my dreams, about possible ways to pin my ears closer to my head, so they didn't protrude that much. My dad said that as I grew, I would grow into my ears, and they would not be so noticeable. He was right, but that event was too far in the future to comfort me.

The self-pity and self-loathing led to a dark melancholy. I began to identify with outcasts in stories and preferred to hear stories of people who were rejected and miserable and who triumphed over their enemies. I began to prefer stories with darker messages, and by middle school, I had become curious about spells and preternatural things like ghosts and spirits. As I recall, this developed alongside my quiet depression and was not something I sought out directly. I was once given a children's book of spells around 5th grade, which was something trivial (not real spells) but which made me very curious about those things. I preferred games that dealt with magic and wanted to learn magic, but I was disappointed when I realized magic tricks were just that – tricks, but without magic. I guess what I was craving was power in the presence of my powerlessness.

The teasing brought with it real enemies. I eventually labeled these bullies as "tormentors" because of the impact their teasing had on me. I took everything very personally and became afraid of many aspects of life. I had very few friends because it was cool to tease the kids that everyone teased, and that was me. In order to keep the friends that I did have, I was willing to be a bit daring about some things, in an effort to impress them.

Still in middle school, I heard about summoning spirits through mirrors,[3] and I heard about kids being scratched by the visions they saw and the idea of selling one's soul to the devil. In my joking around with these things, I expressed a certain openness to these spirits we were discussing, so much so that one day in school, I became terrified that I might have actually sold my soul to the devil based on what I had said out loud among these friends. Thankfully, when a certain sign that was supposed to have happened did not happen, I felt relief that I had not actually done this. However, this event haunted me for the next five years, and it then lingered in the back of my mind for almost 20 more years before I understood it better.

Despite the horror this caused me, my curiosity about these things continued, and in high school, with some friends, I played with a Ouija board and played a levitation game, and likely Tarot cards, all of which the Church, for good reason, tells us to stay away from.

All the while, I was being raised in the Church, though without a good anchor in prayer and moral instruction. I learned morals from my public school more than from the Church, which was disastrous to my spiritual life and my emotions. I had a few moments in middle school and high school where a sense of faith was kindled. I still recall these just as powerfully as the evil things I ventured into. For example, I truly believe it was my Guardian Angel who put an idea,

---

[3] The "Bloody Mary" game, which is basically a form of summoning spirits, and not a game.

of being a "follower of the Messiah," into my head in the eighth grade, and who rescued me from drowning when I was in the ninth grade. I also believe that he was the one who led me into a profound contemplation on life and God's existence as I was trying to fall asleep one night, probably when I was in the fourth or fifth grade. I mention these things because I am nearly certain, as I have looked back more, that God was directly opposing the work of evil in my life, planting seeds and reminders through these powerful events, so I would not drift away too far and would always fear to place myself on a path to Hell.

Since I was raised without knowledge of spiritual warfare, it is only in looking back that I can see I had already been pulled into this battle. I was not fighting, but God was fighting on my behalf until He could get my attention and train me for battle. This He did, though not until my life nearly came to an end.

Chapter Two

Darkness Before the Dawn

My junior year in high school brought a great sense of relief, openness, new friendships, and a bit of real happiness. These new good things quickly became overshadowed by a spiritual storm that began to brew, so to speak, in my senior year. All of the stress, anxiety, and depression which had been unnamed, ignored, and unaddressed – since I never opened up about how bad I perceived things to be, while I processed how miserable I tended to see my life since I was a child – all of that came together for a new and pivotal phase in my life: a stress-induced physical illness and the slow onset of a major depression and a crippling anxiety disorder.

I spent about three months on different diets as the doctors attempted to diagnose the problem. They ruled out everything and concluded it was stress-induced, which, as a result, was difficult to treat. The illness led to a sharp spike in anxiety, as I was a typical over-busy senior in high school, and I could not handle any new stress. I broke up with my girlfriend suddenly and I began to look for ways to escape from the pain, anxiety, and depression. Thankfully, drugs and alcohol did not have a heavy presence in my life just yet. I almost dropped out of high school in my senior year because school had become nearly unbearable. All the while, I managed to be an A/B student and told few people how bad things were.

I went to college and survived the first year. Thankfully, it was filled with less depression and anxiety. This was primarily because college offered new ways to escape from life and I took advantage of some of these. I was simply running very fast away from my problems, but that approach can only last so long.

Remember, too, that God was still not a part of my life in any way. After graduating from high school, I had completely quit going to Mass, which I had <u>never</u> enjoyed. In my youth, I actually felt sick during Mass more often than not, for whatever reason, and often tried to get out of having to go.

Despite a calm first year, at the start of my sophomore year in college everything came crashing down. My anxiety spiked so high that I could hardly leave my apartment. I was nearly paralyzed with anxiety for three hours prior to any class I had to take on campus. Within a couple weeks, I left college on a medical withdrawal. In the next many months, I was diagnosed with social anxiety and major depression, and I was soon on medication for general anxiety, depression, social anxiety, and panic attacks.

I would stay up late into the night processing how meaningless and frightening my life had become. I would sit in my room alone, smoking and drawing the strangest pictures and writing the most depressing poetry trying to "name" the darkness that I was in. The idea of looking into the future with any hope was completely impossible. I blamed God every night for my miseries and for not intervening, as I cried myself to sleep for three months.

But it was at this very moment that my whole world began to change.

Chapter Three

The Divine Intervention Begins

What I didn't know then was that God was actually listening to me. In the middle of this dark time, which encompassed an entire semester of college, a mysterious desire to wear a Cross emerged. It was not a vague desire. I specifically wanted a small wooden Cross, of little monetary value, which would hang from something as basic as yarn or a mere string. I never told anyone about this desire. I went home about two months later for Christmas. One morning, I came downstairs and went over to a table where I would leave my keys. There, sitting next to my keys, I saw a small wooden Cross exactly as I had seen it in my mind. I took it over to my parents to ask them about it but could not even find the words to formulate a question. My mom said, "We thought you might like that." Ok, God, I understand.

That was the first of many signs to come, which I will not have time to describe in detail in this short book.[4] I immediately returned to Mass after a year and a half away and an entire youth of disinterest. I went every Sunday from that point forward, while still suffering from extreme anxiety and depression.

---

[4] See Chapter Eleven, "Stepping into the Light," for a few more stories.

At that same time and that same Christmas while still at home, at the dawn of the year 2000, I happened to see on TV, alone and late at night, Pope John Paul II inaugurate a Jubilee Year, a special year of grace and mercy. Again, at that same time, I suddenly felt a powerful desire to be a priest. I, a practical pagan, completely away from God for many, many years, filled with evil vices and oppressed by anxiety and depression, suddenly wanted to be a priest! This new desire was connected to the thought that had entered my mind in the eighth grade, and which was here resurfacing: to be a "follower of the Messiah." It was as if that eighth-grade idea was now coming to life. This new desire never subsided and guided me for the next 20 years, and still to this day, though it has taken on a different form.

Within two weeks of returning to Church, my therapist, who was an atheist, discovered a new medicine that somehow she had never heard of, and which had, in her own words, the "miraculous side effect" of helping to control the illness I had developed in high school, while also mildly addressing the anxiety and depression. Though it did not take everything away, it gave me a new grip on the entire situation. Over the next six months, I was eventually put on five strong medications to treat these issues.

Those months were a spiritual rollercoaster: I was socially isolated and depressed, taking several prescribed medications and one illegal one, experimenting with the escape routes of the drug culture, and exposed to dangerous people in that same culture. I was nearly arrested once and as close to suicide as I had ever been, without any real friends. All the while, I was trying to feed a desire for God that had introduced itself into my life and refused to be snuffed out, despite the darkness that had engulfed me.

That following summer brought a pivotal moment. One of my few true panic attacks occurred, sparked by driving alone on the interstate, surrounded on all sides by eighteen-wheeler trucks. This panic attack also triggered what the doctor called an "over-medication effect," which made me feel completely "out of it" mentally. At this point, I decided that God had clearly convinced me, over the previous six months, that He alone was my source of peace, and I must rely on Him alone and on nothing else, legal or illegal, to bring me happiness. The reason for this conviction was mysterious to me at the time, but was the secret working of God in my soul, as He prepared to give me a gift that I had never thought was possible.[5]

I slowly got off of all five prescription medications by the following Christmas, and any illegal ones were eliminated by the following Easter. I was also meeting monthly with a group of twelve young men who were also considering the priesthood. That same Easter, just over a year after returning to Mass, they convinced me to return to Confession for the first time since the eighth grade, to begin going to Adoration, and to begin attending daily Mass.

Let me emphasize what was happening. Imagine this scenario: a twenty-year old pagan kid, broken and beaten and frightened and fragile and lost and near despair, suddenly experiences what could be called a "Divine intervention," where God invited Himself into my life with all His power, with my meager and simple "yes." By the time I began attending Daily Mass and regularly going to Confession, it had been a year and a half since my first return to the Church, and had only been about five months since I had begun to feel a little bit better.

The damage was done – from age five to twenty-one – damage, real damage.

---

[5] To be described in the next Chapter.

Chapter Four

The First Gift of the Generous God

Our Lord then initiated a new phase in His work in my life. Just after making my Confession for the first time in seven years – what was truly my first real Confession – God gave this depressed and broken man a gift: supernatural and abundant peace.

I cannot describe it in any other way than by saying that it felt like a form of intoxication, but an intoxication that invigorated me instead of tranquilizing and stupefying me. All around me, I saw and felt God. Whenever I was not talking to someone, I thought of God. I could barely pay attention in my classes at college! I wanted to drop out of college and go follow Our Lord, whatever that entailed. I actually had several conversations with some wise professors and older friends on doing just that.

I had an intense fire of love set within my heart and I could hardly contain myself. People I did not know, when they saw me at daily Mass, would approach me and comment on how happy I looked. I was always smiling. All of this was in spite of the physical illness that I still endured and the clear memory of the darkness from which I had just emerged. All of this was in spite of the fact that I had never thought I could truly be happy, possibly ever in my life, before this moment.

And here is where I began to realize truths about life that I had never known before, and which is the topic I am addressing now: I was in a war. I was a person that Satan and Our Lord were battling for. Satan had me; I was putty in his hands for 20 years. Now, Our Lord had liberated me. He had rescued me and recruited me to follow Him, to run beneath His standard and to take up arms and defend myself and others. I did not really know what spiritual warfare was, but I was about to be taught.

With this peace came dreams, and perhaps this is how Our Lord began my spiritual warfare training. Dreams and dreams and dreams. These were so vivid and so frequent that I began to confuse my dream memory with my waking memory and was often unsure whether a memory was real or dreamed! Our Lord appeared to me in my dreams. The Apostles were with Him. Padre Pio appeared to me. St. Francis appeared to me. Our Lady appeared to me. These were not random and unclear dreams, but ones that taught me how to love Our Lord, how to forgive my tormentors from my past, how to renounce my attachment to earthly things, how to continuously put Our Lord first, and how to suffer as a disciple.

Chapter Five

Binding the Darkness

Take a moment now to pause and reflect on any parts of my story that apply to your life. This is an important point, so please read and consider it carefully. Perhaps you have experienced loneliness, rejection, or isolation, feeling as if you have no true friends. Perhaps you know you are involved in things that risk separating you from God like drugs, evil music, sinful relationships, and anger toward others. Perhaps you feel you have no real faith in your mind, in your heart, and you would prefer to, but you feel there is no way to switch from loving the things of this world, of this culture, to loving the things of God. Perhaps you feel oppressed by a spirit of depression or worthlessness or meaninglessness, of fear or anxiety, and far too often, you have thoughts that try to convince you that leaving this world would resolve and end your sufferings.

Let me first distinguish depression and anxiety from the evil behaviors I have mentioned. Depression and anxiety typically emerge as a result of natural causes and are not sinful. Always approach it this way first: see a doctor or a counselor and try a medication if necessary. It worked for me. My depression and anxiety had natural causes: upon clear reflection, I knew <u>exactly</u> why I was depressed and anxious. At that point, though, Satan can easily prey on our disordered thoughts to make the situation worse. This is simply the devil's typical approach: he leaves no one alone. For me, the depression and anxiety were the beginning of the darkness that enveloped me. The degree to which Satan is involved is difficult to detect, but since he is the Prince of this World and is very active here as a result, it's best to reject any unhealthy or sinful thoughts as if they are <u>somehow</u> tied to Satan's works. The thoughts that flow through the mind of a depressed person are often not healthy, and Satan can take advantage of this situation.

Thoughts like the ones mentioned above dominated my youth, and but for God's secret work in my soul, preparing me for His divine intervention in my sophomore year at college, I would likely no longer be in this world nor able to write this book. Our broken human nature plays a part in all of our sufferings but beyond that, there are two spiritual voices seeking to get our attention: God is one, and Satan is the other. Their voices are clearly distinct, but it requires reflection to separate and name just who is speaking to you when you have certain thoughts.

Here, I want to teach you a simple prayer technique that is effective in repelling the attacks of Satan and his demons. If you know you have a vice (an evil habit), a sin, or a dark repetitive thought like those which someone who is depressed or anxious might hear, think about what that is right now and give it a simple name based on what the thought is or the action is. For example, it could be one of the following: "lust, addiction, doubting God, selfishness, despair, fear, anger, isolation, cutting myself, etc." Now, with that name in mind, pray now:

> "In the Name of Jesus, I renounce [name your vice, sin, or dark thought] and all the times I have embraced it, and I choose obedience to Jesus Christ and His Gospel. In the Name of Jesus, I bind you, spirit of [that same thing] and I cast you to the foot of the Cross to be judged by Our Lord."

Throughout this book, if you are distracted by the burden of one of these things, simply repeat that prayer. If you think of something new, say the prayer against that spirit also.

Chapter Six

What Satan is Doing

I will eventually speak about spiritual warfare more directly, which is what Our Lord was training me for after my conversion, and which He is also training you for, whether you know it or not. Before we get to that, we should discuss briefly just who this enemy is: Satan, a fallen angel.[6]

Satan is a created Angel, technically a Seraph, and was originally the most glorious spirit that God had created. Possessing free will and turning within himself through pride, he made a choice and said, "I will not serve." Then, he and a third of the spirits that God created were cast to the earth by Saint Michael and the holy Angels.

Take note that Satan was not cast into Hell as if into a realm separated from us. He was cast down to this earth and permitted to tempt mankind. Now, he roams the earth as part of God's plan to purify us and make us strong in our faith. Remember, God is good, and He is Goodness itself, so everything He does is ordered toward the good of His children (that's us). Remember this always. It is a core truth of

---

[6] What we know about Satan comes from Sacred Scripture, the Sacred Tradition of the Church, and the experience which the Church has had in opposing him, in the lives of the Saints, and in the work of exorcists.

our Faith. It is also logical and reasonable when you take the time to dwell on this reality.

What is Satan interested in doing?

First, listen to this statement from one of the Church's great Popes, Leo XIII, writing in the year 1884:

13.

> "The race of man, after its miserable fall from God, the Creator and the Giver of heavenly gifts, "through the envy of the devil," separated into two diverse and opposite parts, of which the one steadfastly contends for truth and virtue, the other of those things which are contrary to virtue and to truth. The one is the kingdom of God on earth, namely, the true Church of Jesus Christ; ...The other is the kingdom of Satan, in whose possession and control are all whosoever follow the fatal example of their leader and of our first parents, those who refuse to obey the divine and eternal law..."[7]

Satan is labeled by Our Lord as a deceiver, a liar, and the father of lies, a murderer from the beginning.[8] He plants doubts and lies in the minds of all men and women, beginning with Eve, whom he seduced and convinced to desire what was evil. He encouraged her to follow her own desires and to choose according to her own interests and to disregard God's commands. Satan's deception in his conversation with Eve led her to sin and lose the grace of God and friendship with Him and merit eternal death. As a result, Satan gained authority over them and the earth. Mankind's disobedience toward God, beginning with Adam and Eve, placed us under Satan's dominion.

Think about the temptation Our Lord experienced in the wilderness, when Satan offered Him all the kingdoms of the earth if Our Lord would simply bow down and worship Satan.[9] Think about the number of people who become famous and then become incredibly

---

[7] Humanum Genus. Pope Leo XIII. 1884
[8] John 8:44
[9] Luke 4:7

immoral and godless people afterward. What does it mean to worship Satan? It means to serve his interests, to promote his causes, and to follow his commands. Satan desires the damnation of every human being and prompts us to do what will destroy us.

Chapter Seven

Satan's Plan for Your Life

It is important that you remember, as you go through life, tempted by a variety of evils, that Satan has no interest in your happiness, your pleasure, your enjoyment of life, or your enjoyment of eternal life. Satan wants you to go to Hell. It is a harsh reality, but a reality, nonetheless.

When he turned against God in his beginning, he, as a pure spirit, with an angelic intellect and an angelic will, both of which are more powerful than ours, dedicated himself to one thing: himself, and an attitude of "not God." Satan and all the demons find God revolting. Exorcists teach that when we pray mentally, when we speak to God silently in our minds, it is a powerful weapon against diabolical obsession.[10] Demons will not interact with a mind that is thinking about God. On the other hand, imagine what they can do with a mind that never thinks about God. They can easily guide and ruin that person.

Satan only offers temporal passing pleasures, and those come at the cost of eternal delights! Take note: that's a bad deal! All the sinful things he offers will eventually run out. Earth is the only playground that Satan offers, but death ends that. God promises an

---

[10] One of the extraordinary ways in which the demons tempt us. It is where a demon bombards our minds with evil thoughts and disordered suggestions.

eternal Kingdom that will begin at our passing from this life. There is no question whether we <u>will</u> die – only where we will go once we do.

What Satan offers us also brings death itself. Think about it honestly. "Sexual freedom" brings STDs and unexpected pregnancy with the temptation to commit abortion; excess consumption of foods and drinks leads to illnesses, vomiting, hangovers, stupid choices, addictions, and death itself. Our Lord, on the contrary, calls us to a prudent, careful, and moderate use of the goods of the earth. In the end, following Our Lord's advice keeps us healthy and happy, both on a natural and a supernatural level.

The modern world, with its rejection of God, has given us many witnesses to the true purpose of Satan's works. A famous exorcist told the story of John Lennon of the Beatles, who made a pact with the devil in exchange for 20 years of fame. Almost 20 years to the day from that pact, he was shot and killed. If you look at their work, their albums, both the covers and the lyrics, you will start to see that this may indeed be true.[11] And this is just one example – there are far, far more.

Since we have just mentioned music, let me say this: please be careful with the music you listen to. Again, I teach at a high school, and I investigate what my students are up to. I know the music that is out there. A lot of music is good, and some of it is very good. Still, we must apply moderation to any good thing that we use. However, it is a fact, as we just discussed and which you can research yourself,[12] that many popular bands, over the last 60 years and up to today, embraced a certain aspect of Satanism and filled their music with an attitude that encourages sin, lust, rebellion against any good order, and an attitude of self-before-God. If you think honestly for a moment, you will agree that this is true. How much modern music encourages modesty, respect for authority, purity, waiting for marriage, living for Heaven, etc.? Again, this does not apply to all music.

That being said, music communicates a philosophy and an attitude about life. People sing with passion, and ideas are what inspire

---

[11] Look up the original cover design for the Beatles album "Yesterday and Today" and reflect on the deceptive lyrics of "My Sweet Lord."

[12] The online documentary "Hells Bells 2," while at times graphic and difficult to watch, is very informative on these issues.

passion. So, music is meant to communicate an idea – it's not just a fun rhythm typically. In my high school days, I listened to all of the popular music from Tupac, to Sublime, to Rage Against the Machine, to Nirvana, to Radiohead, to Metallica, etc. I will be honest with you: this music fueled my anger at my life, deepened my depression, and made me very, very curious about drugs. Even in high school before I had any real Christian moral compass, I was aware that some of this music made me want to try drugs, specifically marijuana. I wanted to enter into the experience that the music presented, and that the band seemed to be enjoying.

In college, I slowly began to prefer music that was clearly inspired by drugs like the Grateful Dead, Pink Floyd, Jimi Hendrix, and Led Zeppelin. This fueled my downward spiral and oppressed me in the darkness that I had entered into. I wanted to stay in my misery with this music to keep me company there. These bands and their music, which fueled one or another of my vicious desires, became like a theme song for my life. I would listen to them to escape, or to inflame my anger, or to have a companion in my misery. The music helped enslave me in my doom.

As one priest told me, "God has a plan for your life – Satan has a plan for your life also." Satan seeks to oppose what he knows that God is doing in our lives. He seeks to pervert what God is revealing – distort the truth by defiling it with lies, by allowing inspirations to be discouraged – to lead us into sins so we become wounded. Then, those wounds, like my anger, my anxiety, and my depression, incline us to sin and become the means to control us in life and to keep us obedient to him.

As in the topic of music, which is a good gift that God has placed within the visible world that He created, we can see an important truth: Satan constantly twists and perverts what is good. Every temptation is a perversion of a good. For example: resting, working hard, and being with friends are all good things. But, they can be twisted in a sinful way: resting until you neglect something important; working hard and trying to achieve something based on a false/disordered standard of success; or spending time with your friends even though you know that this means being present for sinful behaviors and conversations, and other temptations.

When a temptation emerges, analyze it, and you will eventually see that there is a good thing being twisted and then presented to you. It may be obvious, or it may be several steps down, but it is there. Taking this time to analyze the temptation will block its initial evil shock and steal some of its power.

Chapter Eight

This Life is a Battlefield

Satan's war is personal for us. Whether or not we are happy about it, we are involved. We are the targets that the demons have in their sights, but we are also soldiers in this war; soldiers who will either fight and be victorious, fight and be killed, or be captured by the enemy, tortured, and converted to his side. The only victory Satan seeks is to steal us from God who has willed and who desires that all mankind is saved and merits eternal life with Him in Heaven. Satan would love to take over the world too, and demons are territorial in that sense, but the reason behind that interest is only to get greater access to us.[13]

Remember the holy and heroic battle that Our Lord Jesus Christ patiently endured from Holy Thursday to Good Friday. This is Our Lord, our King, and our Captain in the battle of the Church against the powers of Hell. He did all of this in order to destroy the power of Satan's Kingdom on earth that we might leave it and enter the Kingdom of Heaven. Remember when Our Lord appointed St. Peter as the head of the Church. He said, "The gates [or powers] of hell will not prevail against it." That is a battle image stating that the Church will wage a direct assault against the Kingdom of Satan, which is operat-

---

[13] This is seen in the work of demons to possess people, obsess our minds, infest homes and buildings, and infiltrate cultures and organizations.

ing on this earth. We, as members of this Church, must pick up our swords and fight as well.

The Church constantly, <u>constantly</u>, calls us to battle. St. Paul says,

> "Do you not know that in a race all the runners compete, but only one receives the prize? So run that you may obtain it. Every athlete exercises self-control in all things. They do it to receive a perishable crown, but we an imperishable. Well, I do not run aimlessly, I do not box as one beating the air; but I pommel my body and subdue it, lest after preaching to others I myself should be disqualified."[14]

Why this great effort? Because, as St. Paul says, we do battle "against the principalities, against the powers, against the world rulers of this present darkness, against the spiritual hosts of wickedness in the heavenly places,"[13] and, as Our Lord says, only "he who perseveres to the end will be saved."[15]

We must acknowledge what sin and Satan have done to us.

It is critical to look and to admit and to face the things that have aligned us with Satan's plan. For me, I believed lies from evil people, and never asked Our Lord what He thought, and I became sheepish and cowardly. I felt anger and consented to it and embraced it, never asking Our Lord how to handle it, and I became tormented internally and raged for revenge. I sought escapes through sinful relationships and compromises with purity[16] and curiosity about drugs, never asking Our Lord to rescue me from a ruined life, and I became isolated and alone and dark, trapped within my own fears and desires. I felt fear and submitted to it and never asked Our Lord to comfort me and calm me, and I became trapped and imprisoned beneath the voices of my tormentors.

This is how Satan sought to destroy my life. These vices and evils oppressed me and lingered in me until I continuously learned and applied the remedies and weapons that the Church gives us in this

---

[14] 1 Corinthians 9:24-27
[15] Matthew 24:13
[16] i.e. chastity and sexual morals

battle.[17] I have seen that some of Satan's attacks are like grappling hooks, not simply spears or darts. By these hooks, he not only wounds us, but he also latches on and hangs around until that specific sin and wound are completely addressed. This causes a sort of spiritual illness, which must be addressed properly.

---

[17] I'll mention these in Chapter Ten and Eleven and the Epilogue, particularly page 41.

Chapter Nine

Opening Our Eyes

So, what must we do to find freedom from the snares and shackles of the enemy of our souls? First, we must confront ourselves and our sins. What is my sin? Why do I like to do that so often? When did this sin begin in my life? Why did I turn to sin and not to God when I was tempted? Do I love this sin or hate this sin? Do I know that I offend God when I sin?   Do I care enough that I offend God when I sin?

We must also confront our work as soldiers – we must honestly ask this: On whose side up until now have I been fighting? What do the deeds of my life reveal? Who is my true Captain?

How demons get to mess with us.

When we sin, Our Lord teaches that we become a slave of the devil. So, take sin seriously! Hate sin – avoid sin – see your weaknesses and predict what your temptations will be. Those weaknesses are precisely where Satan seeks to strike us. Be smart. Saint Paul said, "For freedom Christ has set us free; stand fast therefore, and do not submit again to a yoke of slavery."[18]

Before Satan tries to get you to sin, he tries to get you to think incorrectly, to believe incorrectly, and to perceive the world and others incorrectly. He encourages you to reject what Our Lord has taught, to believe in a vision of morality contrary to what is true, and to distrust others – leading you to "go your own way" and invent your own truth, your own morality, your own reality. Why? This is because that is what Satan himself did! At that point, he then leads you into all the mortal sins that you could possibly commit – intentionally skipping Sunday Mass; lustful behaviors, promiscuity, and pornography; drugs; lying, cheating, and stealing; rejecting the sacramental life of the Church like regular Mass and Confession; blasphemous language; ridicule of the Faith; and refusing to pray to God at all.

Imagine a tree, planted in the ground, about two feet tall, just a sapling. Then, this tree declares that it wants to "do its own thing!" and rips itself out of the ground and begins to walk around. What's going to happen? It is now vulnerable. It is already becoming weak. It will soon begin to wither. Its leaves will fall off. The sap will dry and harden. And it will die. When we sin, we do the same thing. It might be neat to experience something new, fresh air on our "roots" like we've never experienced before, and which those oppressive big trees kept telling us we shouldn't want to do because "it's bad for us!" In a similar way do we need to trust and obey God. He is the foundation for our existence, the Supplier of all our needs and, by abiding by His laws, we stay strong and healthy. But without Him we are vulnerable and will die. Mortal sin makes us vulnerable. It cuts us off from God, and we risk misery here and eternal death to come.

---

[18] Galatians 5:1

Chapter Ten

Take up Your Sword

Once you see the stark reality, and the deceptive and conniving tactics of Satan, how do you fight this war which is spiritual?

First, get into a state of grace if you are not already. Never live in doubt about this – go to Confession regularly. Confession is like a prison break – and the effects are powerful. If you sin and you aren't sure if it was a mortal sin, talk to your priest.

Then, battle temptations. We must renounce Satan, literally, even verbally, and renounce every instance of aligning ourselves with what is actually Satan's plan for us. We must also repeatedly and explicitly choose to be obedient to Jesus Christ.

Think of how you are tempted: what are those thoughts, when do they appear, how are they worded, are there repetitive temptations that reoccur, are they associated with an event or an injury or a sin? Once you diagnose the temptation, be on alert for it, and use the binding prayer to repel this diabolical suggestion.[19]

Pray. Pray. If you never talk to God, it's like you are an AWOL soldier – "absent without leave" – or worse, a deserter. Follow the Captain, follow the King, and pray. A simple reminder of how to

---

[19] See Binding Prayer on pg 16 and the Appendix.

pray well is the word ACTS – Adoration, Contrition, Thanksgiving, Supplication. It works for the young and the old. You may say, "I have some time to pray, but I don't know what to do." ACTS.[20]

Be careful not to embrace harmful expressions and certain popular sayings. When something goes wrong, for example, don't say, "Of course that would happen to me." What's that all about? Do you believe you are cursed?

Analyze the words you use and the thoughts that regularly come into your mind as a response to situations. Are they good? Do they reflect the idea that life is ultimately good, that God loves you, that Heaven is offered to you if you are faithful to God, and that God is ready to forgive you? Or do they reflect, and therefore reinforce, the lie from Satan: that you are worthless, that God has abandoned you, that your life is not worth living, that everything is and always will go wrong in your life?

Think about this in regard to how guilty we feel about sin. For people who think it is unnecessary to go to Confession, they may say something like, "It's not like I killed someone!" Never say this. Confession is for those who do not love God perfectly, not just for murderers!

We often forget what it looks like to love God. Our Lord gave a clear teaching on this, "If you love Me, you will keep My commandments."[21] He also says, "You, therefore, must be perfect, as your heavenly Father is perfect."[22] Saint John, the Apostle, the Beloved Disciple, says, "If we say we have no sin, we deceive ourselves, and the truth is not in us."[23] But, once we live in Christ, in His grace, we begin to sin less and less. We must hate sin in order to love God. Once we begin to hate sin, Our Lord will draw us more and more deeply into Himself, into love, into Truth, into Goodness.

And this will lead to our true happiness.

---

[20] See Epilogue, page 42, for more details
[21] John 14:15
[22] Matthew 5:48
[23] I John 8

Chapter Eleven

Stepping into the Light

It might not be a comforting thing to be told that billions of demons are seeking to devour you and all of your friends and cast them into Hell forever, but sometimes the Truth is unpleasant! So, to brighten things up a bit, let me give you a brief synopsis of some of the great things that Our Lord did in my life once I handed it over completely to Him and embraced His activity in my soul. It wasn't always easy, and it took work, but it also became easier as I grew stronger.

First, as you will recall, God inspired me to desire to wear a Cross – then He gave it to me. When I responded and returned to Mass, He gave me a medicine that actually helped. When I realized that He was my true source of peace, which the medicines first helped me see was even possible, He gave me the courage to rely on Him alone. He gave me a desire for the priesthood, while still quite depressed and burdened. Then He gave me a small group of holy friends who also wanted to be priests. The man with no friends now had some of the best friends imaginable.

My holy spiritual director, whom I had for six years, and who later became a bishop, introduced me to Mother Teresa and St. Francis of Assisi, and I heard the term, "Divine Providence" for the first time.

"Divine Providence" is like a title for God which highlights the fact that God desires to take care of us and provide for all of our needs. This new understanding initiated a "second conversion." My friends taught me the Faith, prayed with me, were honest with me about my sinful habits, took me back to Confession, and then to Adoration, and then to daily Mass. I was now living in a whole new universe, and I knew that I needed to change certain aspects of my life, or I would lose this new and wonderful world.

So, I gave my full, but still weak, "yes" to God. Then Our Lord gave me the intense gift of supernatural peace and made me desire, above all other things, to be a Saint. He gave me vivid and prophetic dreams, special graces to forgive the "tormentors" of my youth, and special graces to pray and seek Him with great courage. I was fueled by a revolutionary spirit of joy, happiness, peace, and excitement about God and life in general.

I worked in parishes for many years as I pursued the priesthood, and I met many holy and intelligent priests who became my mentors and advocates. I battled against opposition and obstacles in my pursuit of seminary and struggled to persevere in the spiritual life, but God, who was ever with me, never let me lose this new peace and joy. Our Lord also spoke to me in extraordinary ways, directing me, and preparing me for hardships He knew were coming.

In seminary, I gained many insights into my life and spiritual life. Our Lord directed me away from the priesthood, and I left seminary having no idea what was next, but truly happier than I had ever been because I knew I was following Our Lord and that He was with me.

I met my future wife four months later without even looking. Mutual friends set us up. She had unknowingly been praying for me, from a seminarian prayer card, for almost two years, mispronouncing my last name every time. We met after Mass on Holy Thursday. We later discovered that the very day in seminary when, through a powerful experience in prayer, I had realized that I was not called to be a priest, my wife was praying as well and experiencing a new sense of hope that God was preparing for her, at that very moment, the man who would be her future husband. We now have three kids who enjoy, most of all, dressing up like nuns and priests and singing Christmas hymns.

A note to introduce the final point before I wrap up: I have always found a spiritual benefit in the use of sacramentals: the St. Benedict medal and crucifix, the Scapular, the Rosary, holy water, and the Miraculous Medal, among others. I highly encourage you to get these and use them. They are physical things which Our Lord has blessed through His Church, and the blessing placed on them flows from Our Lord's love and desire for our salvation.

As a sign to me that God will not be outdone in generosity, while doing research for my book on spiritual warfare,[24] and for this present book as well, and while learning and using certain sacramentals that I had not known about earlier (blessed candles, blessed oil, and blessed salt), God gave me a new extraordinary grace. This was one which, despite all of the other wonderful things that He did in my life, from the first moment of my conversion, He had not yet given to me.

See, He never stops working if you cling to Him.

This grace, and I kid you not, was the grace to see exactly how Satan has been and still is attacking me, the traps he lays for me, the subtle lies he tells me, and how he is still pursuing me in an aggressive way, and an understanding of exactly how I must fight him head on. It has brought abundant new insights and strength to my spiritual life. This new grace, which was given according to God's preferred timing, and by nothing I did, except for my desire for it, arrived right in the middle of my preparations for this book. Think about what that means. Our Lord, who knows me better than I know myself, and who was watching me make a review of my life and the spiritual struggles that it entailed, knew that I was now ready to be shown something new. Not only did He pull back a veil, but He placed a new sword in my hand, so I would be able to fight according to what I would then understand.

I'm not special. He can do the same for you.

---

[24] *Slaying Dragons: What Exorcists See and What We Should Know*

Chapter Twelve

God is Alive, My Friends

As St. Paul said, "Finally, brethren, whatever is true, whatever is honorable, whatever is just, whatever is pure, whatever is lovely, whatever is gracious, if there is any excellence, if there is anything worthy of praise, think about these things. What you have learned and received and heard and seen in me, do; and the God of peace will be with you."[25]

In Baptism, Our Lord invited you to become a friend of God. Confession, the Eucharist, and the other sacraments sustain this. This is the life of joy. Though there is sorrow in life, tough work, and weaknesses to constantly work against, there is joy in the Christian life. Please see my story as an example. I was trapped in the world which presented false standards and condemned me by them; it presented false gods and enslaved me by them; it presented false friends, who encouraged me in my sins; and it brought me to the brink of nothingness and abandoned me there to die. But God is alive, my friends, and He sought me out, despite my sins and despite my lack of interest in Him. He saved me and raised me out of darkness and directed me on the path of light and grace and salvation. I have seen the

---

[25] Philippians 4:8-9

darkness and I lived within it. Our Lord taught me to see the darkness and to fight against it, and He gave me great joy when I said "yes" to Him.

The smile of the Christian drives the devil mad! But that smile must flow from obedience to Almighty God and must be the smile of a Christian soldier, unafraid to suffer in doing what is good. That smile is from the joy that springs up within a soul in friendship with God. God is alive and He is very generous to those who love Him.

Remember from the Gospels, how Our Lord Jesus Christ is so different from everyone else: His wisdom, His peace, His perspective that God is first, how He reacts to things, His strength and confidence when on trial, so much so that Pontius Pilate asks, "Who are You?" These qualities flow from His divinity. Jesus is God. But we become partakers in His divine nature through Baptism.[26] Thus, the potential and the power to be like Jesus is only attainable through Baptism and the life of grace. It cannot be acquired in any other way. Did you know that someone in the Acts of the Apostles actually tried to buy this power from Peter? It didn't work.[27]

So, make a game plan for your life. Pray sincerely and often, fast as much as you are able, and give generously and freely to others. Become holy in Christ. If you are in sin, repent and be restored to grace! Then set your course for Heaven, batting off, with the divine power, with the Sacraments and sacramentals, and with the Name of Jesus, all the pesky little demons that come up against you. Fight, be victorious, and merit the crown of eternal life. Once you win this battle, you will be an eternal victor, ever celebrating, in the presence of Almighty God, and the Angels and the Saints, this victory that Our Lord has brought about in you.

---

[26] 2 Peter 1:4
[27] Acts 8:18ff

Epilogue

What Now?

Hopefully, at this point, you are processing your own life and are becoming aware that...things can change, and perhaps they need to. Sadly, today's youth are exposed to far too many evils and succumb to them. But, as I tell my students – the first part is not your fault. You didn't choose to be born in a generation plagued by so many grave moral evils and pitfalls. Yet, here you are. Some of you will have more wounds than others, some will be graver wounds than others, but none of you are without wounds. The key, now, is that there is something you can do about it.

On that note, don't wait to make a change. As you read in my story, God sought me out and rescued me, despite my lack of interest in Him. I had been consecrated to Him in Baptism, so Our Lord fulfilled His promise and pursued me with His grace. One important thing to state here is: this outcome is not typical. In my life, I have seen more people walk away from God than return to Him. What happened to me is what is called an extraordinary grace. Thus, my admonition here: don't allow your life to get to such a point that it requires God to use such an extraordinary method to get your attention, because it might not happen. It could, but it might not.

So, let's review, and let me add to, what you should consider doing.

Confession. If you have not been to Confession in a while, plan to go as soon as possible. At the back of this book, in Appendix D, there is an "examination of conscience for teenagers." It is both a reflection and an examination. It will be a good guide to help you reflect on your sins. There are others that you can also find online. This will help you become more aware of all the times that you have sinned so you can name these deeds in the presence of God and receive His forgiveness. Even though you may have forgotten a deed from your past, it is still a reality that must be confronted. Remember: Confession is like a prison break! Do it.

Honesty. Be honest with yourself. You know, deep down, what sin is. You know, in your conscience, that some things are wrong. Face that fact. Name your sins. Then renounce them.

Binding prayer. Use the binding prayer[28] and renounce the temptations as they come against you. Renounce also all of those times that you gave in to that sin. Renounce lies that you believed. Renounce things you may have said. Renounce any evil thing you can remember that you did. Then, use the binding prayer regarding those specific sins. You will gain new insights about yourself by this process. Afterward, you will also know better what you should be confessing.

Start praying. Don't worry about what to say as much as actually saying something. Make it intentional, though. Pick a time when you can be alone. Speak to Our Lord from the heart. Tell Him your burdens. Ask Him for what you really need. Know that He is listening. Then, make this a daily habit. Prayer becomes easier and easier the more you pray. Use a combination of memorized prayers and prayers in your own words. Then consider looking for a good prayer book.

Sinful habits. If you are aware of certain sinful habits that you have, admit to yourself that you have to cut them out of your life as soon as

---

[28] See Appendix A and page 16.

possible. Though it may entail a radical change in your life, there truly is no justification to delay.

Your music. Pause and turn off your music for a moment. Make an
inventory of the albums you listen to regularly. Are any of them vulgar? Do any celebrate sin, impurity, rebellion, or violence? Do any
of the bands invoke the occult or Satanic imagery or references? Do
the melodies cause you to become agitated or angry or depressed? If
any of them are clearly leading you in a direction that opposes virtue
and human dignity and man's pursuit of what is good, be brave and
toss them in the trash.

Talk to devout Catholics. Think about the people you know who are
devout Catholics. Is there a parent or a friend you know? Are you
able or comfortable speaking to your priest? Pick someone who is
knowledgeable about the Catholic Faith. One benefit is that they can
help you acquire holy water and other sacramentals, as well as answer
your questions. When you go to Confession, that would be a good
moment, for example. Ask this priest to help you acquire some holy
water. Typically, it is not too difficult to find a small bottle designed
to hold holy water. Take this home and use it regularly in your home,
your room, your car, and to bless yourself whenever you desire, particularly before sleep.

Get your house blessed. Talk to your parents if you live at home and
see if your house has been blessed by a priest. If not, have that done
as soon as possible. Simply call the Church office and ask to sched-
ule the priest to come over for a meal and to bless the house. It is a
standard thing for a priest to do, so don't be worried about that.

Sacramentals. Acquire all the sacramentals, as you are comfortable.
Ask the priest to enroll you in the Scapular. He will know what to do
and can explain it to you. It is a simple but powerful devotion to Our
Lady and involves wearing a small piece of brown cloth on strings
like a necklace. It has a special blessing on it and Our Lady has given
many promises to those who wear it. You can attach a Miraculous
Medal and a Saint Benedict Medal to the Scapular. These also have
special blessings on them. Again, the priest will know what to do.

Blessed salt, blessed oil, and blessed candles are also important and helpful sacramentals. I highly encourage you to incorporate all of these into your life, but take your time and ask a good priest how to proceed.

How to pray. When you pray, remember ACTS. Begin with Adoration, praising God for His goodness, patience, mercy, power, generosity, etc. Think of how He made the world, the goodness of the world, how He made you, and your dignity. Repent and ask forgiveness for breaking any of His divine laws which you are aware of having broken. His laws correspond with our nature and are meant to protect our life and our dignity and our eternal destiny. Thank Him for anything and everything that comes to mind. God desires that we have gratitude for the good things that He gives us. Our thankfulness also disposes God to hear our prayers and answer them more generously. Then, at the end, ask Him for anything and everything that you or your loved ones need, and which corresponds to His will, as best as you understand it.

Devotion to Our Lady is key. Nurture a devotion to the Blessed Virgin Mary through the Holy Rosary and under the titles "Our Lady of Sorrows" and "Our Lady, Undoer of Knots." Our Lady has many titles, which can be found in the Litany of Loreto.[29] Each title is there for a specific reason and highlights a specific aspect of the mission which Our Lord has given to His mother. A devotion to Mary is vital for us because, as Scripture says, she is our Mother. The Immaculate Mother of God is also <u>our</u> Mother. Jesus gave her to all of His disciples when He was dying on the Cross. She is the Queen with her Son Jesus the King. Therefore, she has authority in Heaven and God listens to her prayers in a special way.

"Our Lady of Sorrows." This title for the Blessed Virgin Mary highlights the pain and anguish which Our Lady endured as the Mother of the Redeemer. Partaking in His sufferings in such a unique way, as she alone was able to do, enabled her to receive from God particular insights into His plan for our salvation. Her acceptance of her

---

[29] Easily found online.

Son's mission, including His death, brought her into an intimacy with Our Lord which no one else could experience. Through this, she has been given knowledge regarding our spiritual struggles and can show us the real source of our spiritual weaknesses.

"Our Lady, Undoer of Knots." This is a title that reflects Mary's role as the New Eve. What Eve bound, through her sin and disobedience, Mary released, through her faithfulness and obedience. As a result, she can help us undo the bondage and restrictions we experience as a result of our personal sins and help us experience the freedom which Our Lord desires to give us through His grace.

Analyze the way you think. Avoid thinking in a way where you put yourself down, predict there will be disaster after disaster, think other people don't like you, that you are not good enough for your friends or for your parents, that you will never amount to anything, that "life's just too hard" or "I just can't do this." Much of our negative thinking emerges from the lie that we are all alone in this life and that we cannot trust others or entrust our fears and dreams and cares to others. When you realize you are thinking something that is a lie like these listed here, use the binding prayer against the "spirit of _____." It can be phrased as simply as the "spirit of 'I can't do this'" or the "spirit of 'nobody cares about me'."

The Holy Name of Jesus. Invoke the Holy Name of Jesus whenever you feel fears or worries or unbearable burdens or depressing situations or that you are tempted to return to your old sins. Simply say something like, "O Jesus, help me, I trust in You." That will be enough in that moment. Speak to Him at length when you have time.

The reality of Satan. How do we know Satan is real? If "look around" is not a good enough answer for you at the moment, then look at the Gospels. Despite what skeptics try so hard to believe, Jesus Christ is a real historical figure and the Gospels are accurate historical accounts of everything that happened. Most honest atheists today even admit as much. In the two thousand year history of the Church, countless Saints, like Our Lord in the Gospels, have fought the devil face to face, and not simply by resisting temptations: St.

Jean Vianney, St. Padre Pio, St. Teresa of Avila, St. Francis of Assisi, St. Anthony of the Desert, St. Dominic, St. Gemma Galgani, and St. Benedict of Nursia, just to name a few. Their lives are not fiction – it really happened. Do some research and you'll be amazed.

Wounds. Think about your life and the major wounds that you carry. Do these wounds come from family drama, friends, disappointments, relocation, drugs, mistakes, failures, injuries, a sense that God does not love you, etc.? Take some time alone and reflect and be honest. You need to know what wounds you are carrying in your soul. Satan can play on these wounds and push you around by them. You will also realize that, often, some specific actions that you do spring from these wounds. The way you respond to people, what you expect to happen, what you want and desire, what you feel you deserve, what you feel you will never get, how you feel when certain things happen or don't happen, etc. – all of these can be impacted by the wounds you carry.

Practical thing – food. On a very practical level, take a look at what you eat. If you are eating a lot of candy and fat, it could easily have a negative impact on your mood and the way you feel about things. Just cut back on unhealthy foods and eat more healthy foods. It's pretty simple and will have a noticeable impact. If you are anxious or depressed, take a look at the amount of sugar and caffeine you consume. These two can greatly heighten the level of anxiety you feel, which can sometimes cause an increase in how depressed you feel later on.

Improve your mood. Do things that are proven to boost your mood, like exercise, fresh air, quiet, and a good book. At some moments, caffeine can also boost your mood, which is a good thing. Just use moderation so it doesn't make you anxious.

Ask for help. If you find that you need help making changes in your life in order to break free from dangerous ways of living or thinking, ask for help. There are many good people out there who actually have very helpful wisdom to offer. Trust me, I've been there.

Appendix B

Prayer to Our Lady of Sorrows

O Blessed Virgin Mary, Mother of our Redeemer! remember we are thy children, given to thee by thy Divine Son, when expiring on the cross. Mother of sorrows! by the tears which flowed from thy eyes when Saint John related how the traitor Judas sold thy Divine Son for the vile price of thirty pieces of silver; how, in the Garden of Olives, he was agonized with fear and sorrow, the blood gushing through every pore; by all the anguish that overwhelmed thy heart when thou didst hear that Jesus, the only object of thy love, was condemned to death; by the sorrow that pierced thy maternal bosom, in meeting thy only beloved Son loaded with a heavy cross, spent through loss of blood, fatigue and pain; by that heroic resignation to the divine will, which, triumphing over the sentiments of nature, sustained thee at the foot of the cross; by the excess of grief that would have robbed thee of life, had not God preserved thee for the comfort of his disciples and of his infant church; by the dolors that rent thy desolate heart when beholding thy beloved Jesus, most beautiful in his comeliness above the sons of men, become a prey to death, the ignominious death of the cross; by all the sufferings of thy most afflicted heart, obtain for us, O Mother of Mercy, true contrition for our sins, persevering fervour in the divine service, and the particular favours we solicit in this Novena.

O thou most tender and afflicted Mother, who didst sacrifice thyself on the same altar with thy beloved Son, and whose heart was penetrated by the nails that fastened him to the cross; as it was our sins inflicted those torments on thy Divine Son, we acknowledge that we justly deserve the wrath of divine justice to fall on our devoted heads. But if those very sufferings have proved our defence and protection heretofore, grant that now at least we may participate profoundly in the sorrow of which we have been the unhappy cause; and obtain, that souls hitherto so insensible to the strongest proofs of love, may, by heartfelt contrition, taste one drop of that bitter chalice of which thou didst drink so deeply.

Amen.[30]

---

[30] This prayer comes from the great website https://www.praymorenovenas.com

Appendix C

Prayer to Our Lady, Undoer of Knots

Virgin Mary, Mother of fair love, Mother who never refuses to come to the aid of a child in need, Mother whose hands never cease to serve your beloved children because they are moved by the divine love and immense mercy that exist in your heart, cast your compassionate eyes upon me and see the snarl of knots that exists in my life. You know very well how desperate I am, my pain, and how I am bound by these knots. Mary, Mother to whom God entrusted the undoing of the knots in the lives of his children, I entrust into your hands the ribbon of my life. No one, not even the evil one himself, can take it away from your precious care. In your hands there is no knot that cannot be undone. Powerful Mother, by your grace and intercessory power with Your Son and My Liberator, Jesus, take into your hands today this knot. [*Mention your request here*] I beg you to undo it for the glory of God, once for all. You are my hope.

O my Lady, you are the only consolation God gives me, the fortification of my feeble strength, the enrichment of my destitution, and, with Christ, the freedom from my chains. Hear my plea. Keep me, guide me, protect me, o safe refuge! Mary, Undoer of Knots, pray for me. Amen.[31]

---

[31] This prayer comes from the great website https://www.praymorenovenas.com

Appendix D

Examination of Conscience for Teenagers

There are many good examinations of conscience available online, in books, and in parishes. They are traditionally based on the Ten Commandments and list many sins or reflection questions to help you understand what you may have done that is offensive to Our Lord. We are weak creatures and this weakness leads to several problems. First, it leads us to choose to do things that appear to be good but which the Church and our conscience tell us is not good. Second, it makes us unable to see clearly those things which are sinful in the eyes of God. Finally, it leads to a difficulty in remembering the times we have sinned and the specific sins we have committed. This is why an examination of conscience is so helpful.

The following examination of conscience is written based on traditional approaches while also taking into consideration the observations I have made as a high school Theology teacher for eight years. It is brief, with the intention of helping you begin to critically analyze the state of your soul and where you need to begin the spiritual work necessary to find freedom in Christ.

First, take a moment and reflect on this fact: you are a creature whom the Almighty Creator fashioned with His power and upon whom He bestowed a great dignity and an even greater potential dignity in Christ. He placed within you an immortal soul, capable of distinguishing right from wrong. He entered this world to establish His Church so that all mankind will be able to clearly distinguish what is good and what is bad and have the strength and grace and courage to always do what is right. This same Church was also similarly established for the purpose of rescuing mankind who had gone astray and was lost and broken. The mercy of God is poured out upon the world through His Church. You must cling to Him in His Church, as He willed. If you do so, you will become holy, strong, joyful, hopeful, courageous, wise and, after your death in God's grace, you will be glorified and given eternal peace and life with God.

To do that, you must name your sins, renounce your sins, turn away from your sins, repent and confess your sins, do penance, deny your earthly cravings, be formed in the image of Our Lord, and love and do only what is good. This means you must change. This change began in Baptism, but it truly bears fruit when you are finally serious about God and align your will with His will. This change bears full fruit when you are able to purge the defects from your intellect and will, freeing yourself from the lies of Satan, that you may love according to the mind of God.

To do that, you must call yourself out, so to speak, by naming your sins in the presence of the priest of Jesus Christ. When he absolves you of your sins, you will experience a surge of confidence in the love and mercy of God – this is a true grace that He bestows, particularly in the beginning of your return to Him. You will also experience special graces to aid you in overcoming these weaknesses, so you will not repeat your sins.

This is a process, of course, and it may take longer for some to turn around than for others, depending on how deep one has gone into a life of sin. Regardless, God can turn any one of us into a Saint, despite your past, if you cooperate with Him and let Him do that work in your soul. Thus, this requires your cooperation. You must both 1) work against your weaknesses and vow never to repeat those sins again and 2) rely on the graces of God that come through prayer, the Sacraments, the sacramentals, and the intercession of the Angels and Saints. You cannot do this alone. The more you depend on these things, the stronger you will become.

Examination of Conscience for Teenagers

Note this reality: God <u>actually gives</u> real and tangible and supernatural graces to you which will make you stronger, purer, wiser, and holier. God <u>can</u> change you, if you cooperate.

Those things being said, as you prepare to make a Confession, even if it is simply a weak thought in your mind at the moment, and you have not decided to go just yet, please read the following reflection and consider the sins which you carry in your soul at this moment. As you read, know that God is ready and willing to forgive every single one of them, regardless of how evil those deeds are and of how much shame you feel at having committed them.

~~~~~~~~~~~~~~~~~~~~~~

Have I assisted another in their sins, by praising their sin, commanding them to sin, encouraging them to sin, counselling them to sin, not stopping them from sinning when it was possible to do so, joining them in their sin, or by protecting those who do evil?

Have I disrespected my parents?

Have I disobeyed my parents?

Have I used vulgar or violent language toward my parents?

Have I mocked the Faith in speech or action or gesture?

Have I mocked others for their devotions and personal piety or religious behavior?

Have I taken the Name of the Lord in vain?

Have I listened to music which uses vulgar, violent, sexual or Satanic language or language which speaks against God and the life of virtue?

Have I used Ouija boards, Tarot cards, or any other occult means of divination or recourse to Satanism, magic or magical influences?

Have I been impure with myself or others through deeds such as intercourse, sodomy, masturbation, or any other sexual stimulation with myself or another?

Have I looked at pornography?

Have I taken and/or sent to others nude photos of myself or someone else?

Have I consented to impure thoughts and fantasies?

Have I used impure language or encouraged others in their use of impure language?

Have I watched impure movies or shows?

Have I dressed immodestly or in a provocative manner? Have I done so with the intention of leading another into sin?

Have I lied? Have I done so deliberately and with the intent to deceive or harm others?

Have I stolen anything? Have I done so without making restitution?

Have I gossiped about another person? Have I done so with the intention of ruining their reputation?

Have I consumed alcohol underage?

Have I consumed alcohol to the point of intoxication?

Have I used illegal drugs?

Have I used prescription drugs contrary to the purpose for which they were prescribed, particularly if they were not prescribed to me?

Have I attempted to harm another person? Have I harmed another person?

Have I encouraged another to have an abortion? Have I helped them in any way to acquire an abortion?

Have I attempted suicide or otherwise sought to harm myself?

Have I cut myself on purpose?

Have I intentionally placed myself in a dangerous situation which could have led to my death?

Have I taken pills or drunk to excess with the intention of permitting death to follow without a desire to seek help?

Have I despaired of God's love?

Have I denied that I was Catholic?

Have I denied the existence of God?

Have I spoken openly against a teaching of the Church?

Have I denied the authority of the Church and the fact that she was founded by Our Lord?

Have I abandoned the practice of the Faith for a period of time?

Have I received Holy Communion in a state of sin?

Have I been negligent or disrespectful at Mass, such as by not paying attention, arriving late, leaving early, or mocking aspects of the Mass while present in the pew?

Have I refused to do what the Church commands us to do, such as Sunday Mass attendance and minimal yearly Confession?

Have I neglected the command to rest on Sunday by doing unnecessary servile work on Sunday, like homework, school projects, or athletic competitions?

Have I spent my free time on Sunday doing things contrary to the spirit of the day, such as watching immoral movies and forms of entertainment contrary to the sacred rest commanded by God?

Have I refused to do what is necessary for my soul and aids my spiritual growth, such as daily prayer, regular Confession, acts of piety, works of mercy, frequent reception of Holy Communion, etc.?

About the Author

Charles D. Fraune was the founding Theology teacher of Christ the King Catholic High School in Huntersville, NC and has been a Theology teacher there for eight years. In addition, he has taught nearly every grade level, from second grade to adult, including on the college and Diocesan level. He spent three semesters in seminary with the Diocese of Raleigh at St. Charles Borromeo Seminary in Pennsylvania. This completed a nine-year discernment of the priesthood and religious life after which he discerned that Our Lord was not calling him to the priesthood. He has a Master of Arts in Theology from the Christendom College Graduate School, as well as an Advanced Apostolic Catechetical Diploma. His enjoyment of writing began over twenty years ago, and finally culminated in his first completed book, *Come Away By Yourselves*. In addition to this, he has been working on books related to various aspects of the Catholic Faith, and to the powerful story of his return to the Catholic Faith after a time struggling with illness and depression. Charles is also a dedicated "backyard farmer." He lives in the Diocese of Charlotte, NC with his wife and three young children.

To our readers

We would like to hear from our readers.

Comments, questions, suggested topics for additional books, etc.

Send us an email at retreatmaster@theretreatbox.com.

Printed in Great Britain
by Amazon